ITALIAN HOME COOKING

*Authentic Italian Home Cooking Made Easy
(2023 Guide for Beginners)*

Chloe Allen

CONTENTS

INTRODUCTION

The menu is the quickest way to recognize and fall in love with Italy.

Italian food takes pleasure in simple, flavorful pairings of the healthiest ingredients. Each region is fortunate to have its goods, traditional recipes, and regional specialties. Dining is a social experience in which family and friends come to share tales, laugh together, and like each other's company as well as the delicious meal. Italian cuisine has a history of meals based on starchy foods (such as bread and pasta), grains, cheese, seafood, and beef, often cooked to preserve their products' good qualities, beauty, and flavor.

This cooking style stresses liveliness and healthy eating using organic, unadulterated products. It varies greatly depending on the climate and geography of the country.

Mountainous areas enjoy protein-rich cuisines like beef, cheese, and butter, whereas seaside areas prefer vegetables and fish. The constancy of the products is the first thing to notice about Italian food. Italians take great care of the flavor of their products and employ basic cooking methods to increase the meal's flavor enhancers. That is why, in practically all classic Italian restaurants, meals change quarterly or even daily, depending on which vegetables are in season or which fish was caught that day. The next thing to remember about Italian food is that it does not exist. Italian cuisine is quite regional; each part of the country makes something that no other region does. This is partly due to the world's concise history as a single nation and the fact that different locations cultivate different crops and have different animals.

Due to its peasant beginnings, classic Italian cuisine is simple.
Individuals working full-time and with little resources might use the culinary methods described there. This describes the absence of recipes containing components that necessitate prolonged, close attention and precise temps, such as a delicate cookie or fine spices.

There are plenty of other fascinating aspects of Italian cuisine.

"Italian Home Cooking" is a cookbook that organizes Italian cuisine. It is divided into five chapters. The first chapter briefly introduces Italian cuisine, split into regions.

Northern Italy, Central Italy, and Southern Italy are the three main regions of Italy. Northern Italian recipes are found in Chapter 2, while Central Italian and Southern Italian foods are found in Chapters 3 and 4. The fifth chapter is all about Italy's famous cuisine. Begin reading this book to discover more about Italian cuisine and famous recipes from around the country.

Chapter 1: A Quick Look at Italian Food

Italian cuisine is incredibly diverse. Each of Italy's twenty regions has its own set of flavors, cuisines, goods, and products. In truth, the Italian regions were fully united as a nation in the mid-nineteenth century, so each sovereign province retained much of its heritage. Italy is one of the world's major wine producers, producing red and white varietals. Italy has a broad regional diversity of excellent bread and pasta dishes. Italian bread varies widely in size, flavor, and texture.

The national definition of the framework of classic meals unites Italy. Instead of cooking everything in one or two pieces, Italian meals frequently consist of multiple little dishes served sequentially, giving customers a long time to savor food and service. Dessert is frequently served at the end of a delicious meal but is also commonly consumed alone as an afternoon snack. Today, a considerably more comprehensive variety of pizzas can be found throughout Italy. On the other hand, the classic pizza represents the exquisite elegance inherent in Italian cuisine.

1.1 The Intriguing History of Italian Cuisine

Although Italian food had become intricate and diversified by the end of the Roman era, it had begun rather simply. However, Italy was not the boot-shaped united nation we know today. It was a mash-up of many locations, cultures, and dishes. For example, the Sicilians were known for producing the best cheese. Various items were also produced in other parts of the Empire, such as Gaul and Greek (modern-day France), and brought to Rome. Even after the Roman Empire fell, Sicilian cuisine remained excellent.

Outsiders have visited Italy at various times throughout its history. German and Austrian immigrants from the other side of the world have influenced cooking. Italian cuisine is well-known for its heavy usage of tomatoes. The early modern Italian food period was inspired by the sites of Rome, Florence, Ferrara, and Venice, which were vital aspects that led to the creation of exquisite cuisine in Italy. The new age saw a considerable diversification of Italian food, and during the 18th and 19th centuries, what is now known as Italy was dominated by Spain, France, and Austria. At the end of the 18th century, Italian cooks began to describe the real regionalism of Italian food to exhibit the pride of their territories rather than the high gastronomy of Spain, France, and Austria. The cuisine's scale, importance, and intensity grew as the year progressed.

Throughout the 18th century, families ate a diet of hard grain. As a move towards Italy's high cuisine, which was more refined and fragile, this dish gave the farmers their moniker. Many farmers had to survive by eating decaying food and damp bread. There are numerous reasons why food in Italy varies greatly depending on where you go. While you can get famous pizza and pasta dishes everywhere, the food varies greatly if you wander off the beaten path a little. Italy was never genuinely Italian, particularly in the South Tyrol and Dolomites regions. These persons were originally Austrian until the conclusion of World War II. That's why everyone up there appears to be fluent in German. The popularity of Italian food can be attributed in part to the significant immigration of Italians to North America, the United Kingdom, and other parts of Europe.

1.2 Historical Information and Traditional Italian Cuisine

Beautiful Italy welcomes visitors who want to enjoy its wonderful nature, rich history, and gastronomic delights. With its diverse gastronomic offerings, this charming Mediterranean country provides many popular and traditional must-eat items. If you're in Italy, many famous International delicacies and dishes, sweet and savory, await your research. These traditional Italian foods are deeply established in the history of Italy, and recipes are usually passed down through families and valued for their authenticity. Here are some fascinating facts regarding Italian cuisine.

Italians do not eat meatballs with their spaghetti. The average Italian consumes more than 51 pounds of pasta each year. The average North American consumes approximately 15.5 pounds each year. Over 600 pasta shapes are produced worldwide. However, Italian kitchens only used tomato sauce for spaghetti in the 18th century.

Pizza was invented in Naples in the 18th century. In most Italian homes, the supper table includes water, wine, and bread. A famous wedding soup is not Italian wedding soup. It suggests that the meat and vegetables work well together. Most Italians consume pasta at least once each day. Lunch is the main meal of the day in Italy. Lunch is known as "il pranzo." Italy finished second in the world in winemaking, trailing only France and ahead of the United States and Spain.

1.3 Regional Italian Cuisines

The regions of Italy have specific gastronomic rituals that reflect their history and culture, separating them from the country as a whole. Southern, middle, and northern Italy's culinary regions can be divided into three categories. Italian food includes Bistecca alla Fiorentina in central Italy, Risotto in the north, and pizza in the south. Italy's kingdoms were established in the 1860s, and the State of Italy was established after the Second World War, resulting in regional cultures and customs unique from broader Italy.

Italy's 20 regions showcase its rich culinary tradition, with individuals using new, natural, and seasonal products. With exclusively locally available ingredients, Italy's regions have preserved their culinary heritage and the characteristics of traditional regional recipes. Some localities in Italy have gastronomic analogies based on shared cultural backgrounds, depending on their location. Northern Italian regions generally employ butter in popular meals, but southern Italian regions prefer butter over olive oil. Although the prevalent misunderstanding of Italian cuisine portrays pizza, meatballs with spaghetti, and spaghetti Bolognese as typical dishes worldwide, Italian food by region is far more extensive and historically and culturally defined.

1.4 Italian Cuisine's Geographical Influences

The climate and natural environment have significantly impacted developing regional varietals. Smooth risotto and other exquisitely scented foods are famous in the Northern regions, while the vibrant South is known for its rich olive oil and tomato-based cuisine. Meat is best consumed in Tuscany as Florentine sausages from selected cattle raised in the Chianina

Valley. Alba and the surrounding Piedmont districts produce expensive truffle mushrooms, particularly aromatic white fritters. Fresh fish is robust and diversified throughout the peninsula due to its proximity to the Adriatic and Mediterranean Seas.

The locality is so essential for many Italian culinary items that laws exist to safeguard the quality of products produced in a specific location. Pasta differs from one location to the next. New handmade pasta is famous throughout Italy, and it is always served lightly garnished to prevent overpowering its delicate flavor. Dried pasta is the most prevalent in the South and can be adorned creatively. Some argue that Italy has considerably more pasta varieties than one person could devour in a lifetime. Italians were spotted arguing about a specific pasta shape's full nomenclature and culinary application.

1.5 Making Homemade Italian Food

Nutrition is a secondary priority when it comes to Italian food. A classic Italian lunch starts with a huge plate of antipasti, which consists mainly of vegetables (such as pepperoncini, artichoke hearts, and mushrooms) and grilled meat. Then there's a tiny pasta dish with a lighter protein, like a leg of lamb, cooked simply but delectably. It becomes easier as the meal progresses. Italian dinners tend to build to a climax.

Ingredients That Are Required

Most Italian dishes begin with olive oil, followed by vegetables. The traditional suspects are onion and garlic, but the plate's stars are bright green vegetables. Balsamic vinegar still has a prominent place in Italian cuisine, and you'll need help finding a chef who still needs a slice of Grana Padano on hand. The Italians love preserving food, turning bacon into salami and sausage, grapes into wine, and onions into pickled vegetables. They are firm believers in putting up the effort to preserve the deliciousness.

Nutritional Information

Many new Italian appetizers are created using savory vegetables such as tomatoes, sweet potato, and eggplant and healthy oil sources such as olives or canola oil. If you keep the serving sizes small, you can enjoy a vegetable soup or antipasto salad, a tiny pasta part, and a fatty protein and veggie main. Unsurprisingly, the starchy, puffy pasta seen on most Italian menus will only do a little for your waistline. The nutrition of Italian food is also affected by where you dine. Italian cuisine tends to be high in carbs due to the addition of spaghetti, while certain low-carbohydrate options may exist. The specific nutritional criteria change depending on the ingredients.

Tools

Italian food has always excelled in producing a superb dining experience for all of its devotees. If you enjoy cooking excellent Italian cuisine, you will need the proper tools.

Ladle
Baking dish
Spoon made of wood
The chef's knife
grater for cheese
The garlic press
Colanders

Recipes from Northern Italy, Chapter 2

2.1 Recipes for Appetisers and Breakfast

Torte de Brunch Northern Italian

1 hour 50 minutes to cook
12 portion size

Ingredients:
1/2lb provolone cheese
2 roasted delicious red pepper jars
1/2lb deli ham
1/2lb hard salami
2 crescent roll tubes
2 tsp. Italian seasoning
1/8 teaspoon black pepper
1 tablespoon of olive oil
7 big eggs
1 cup Parmesan cheese, grated
1 cup sliced fresh mushrooms
1 pound fresh baby spinach

Method:

1. Preheat the oven to 350°F. Place the 9-inch greased dish on top.
2. Tightly wrap the foil around the plate. Unroll 1 sheet of crescent dough and cut it into triangles.
3. Push on the prepared plate's bottom to shape a surface, sealing the seams carefully. Once set, bake for another 10-15 minutes.
4. In the meantime, heat the oil in a big pan over medium heat.
5. Stir in the mushrooms and vegetables and simmer until the mushrooms are soft.
6. Blot well after draining on a couple of paper towels. Combine the six eggs, grated cheese, Italian seasoning, and peppers in a large mixing bowl.
7. Divide the crust into 7 pieces and top with salami, ham, provolone cheese, bell peppers, and spinach.
8. Pour a portion over the beaten egg. Layers should be repeated; cover with a combination of remaining whites.
9. Unroll the remaining crescent pastry and cut it into triangles on a cutting board.
10. To form a ring and seal the edges, press them together and place them across the filling. Brush the remaining eggs over the dough.

11. Bake, exposed, for 1 hour, or until the thermometer reads 160°, loosely wrapped in foil to prevent over-browning.
12. Gently loosen the edges of the pan with a knife; remove the pan's rim. Allow for 20 minutes of standing time.

Cloud Eggs from the Northern Italian Alps

Time to cook: 25 minutes
Size of each serving: 4

Ingredients:
1 tablespoon fresh basil, minced
1 tsp. sun-dried tomatoes
four huge eggs
1/8 teaspoon black pepper
1/4 cup Parmesan cheese, shredded
1/8 teaspoon of salt
1/4 tsp Italian seasoning

Method:
1. Preheat the oven to 450°F.
2. Separate eggs; place whites and yolks in four small primary dishes in a large pot.
3. Whisk together the egg whites, Italian spices, salt, and pepper until stiff peaks form.
4. Drop the egg white mixture into four mounds in a nine-inch cast-iron skillet well coated with cooking oil.

5. Using the slotted spoon, make a shallow well in the center of each mound.
6. Sprinkle with cheese. Bake for about five minutes or until golden brown.
7. Gently press an egg yolk into each of the mounds.
8. Bake for 3-5 minutes or until the yolks are set.
9. Scatter with basil and tomato. Immediately serve.

2.2 Recipes for Snacks and Lunch

Stew of Northern Italian Beef

Time to cook: 4 hours 50 minutes
Size of each serving: 8

Ingredients:
1-quart beef broth
2 tablespoons tomato sauce
2 tbsp of olive oil
1 teaspoon fresh marjoram
1/2 teaspoon of sage
1 teaspoon basil
1 teaspoon fresh thyme
four big tomatoes
1/2 lb red potatoes
2-pound top round lean
2 tbsp minced garlic
2 cups red wine, dry

four big carrots
1lb cremini mushrooms
2 medium sweet onions
2 cups celery chunks

Method:
1. Heat the olive oil over medium heat in a large pan.
2. Cook beef in batches in heated oil until thoroughly golden brown, about five minutes per unit.
3. Transfer cooked beef cubes to a sheet lined with towels, keep the skillet warm, and save the cooking liquid.
4. Cook and stir the cabbage, celery, and vegetables in the remaining beef cooking liquid for two or three minutes or until tender.
5. Combine the onion, garlic, and mushrooms in a mixing bowl.
6. Pour in the red wine and boil with a spoon while brushing the browned pieces of food from the pan's sides.
7. Cook the mixture for another 10 to 15 minutes or until the wine has evaporated.
8. Combine the tomatoes and the solution.
9. Return the steak to the pan with the tomatoes, garlic, thyme, marjoram, and herbs.
10. Pour the beef reserve and tomatoes over the mixture.

11. Bring it and the liquid to a boil.
12. Reduce the heat to medium-low and cook for four to six hours or until the meat is tender and the gravy is thick. Serve hot.

Loaded Fries from Northern Italy

Time to cook: 40 minutes
Servings per container: 10

Ingredients:
5 pound straight cut gold fries
28 ounces zucchini
10 tbsp fresh basil
30 ounces tomato sauce
5 ounces of parmesan cheese
1 teaspoon garlic
1-quart olive oil
1 teaspoon black pepper
Cremini mushrooms (28 oz.)
a teaspoon of salt

Method:
1. Heat the olive oil over medium heat in a large pan.
2. Add the zucchini and mushrooms until the vegetables are cooked but still solid.
3. Stir in the garlic, then season to taste. Keep it warm and set it away for work.

4. Begin by making 8 ounces of fries for each section according to the package recommendations.
5. Season with salts. Put the service layer on top of a warmed one.
6. Top with three fluid ounces of warmed tomato sauce and four ounces of sautéed vegetables.
7. Garnish with half an ounce of Parmesan and one tablespoon of fresh basil. Simply serve.

Excellent Northern Italian Lasagne

Time to cook: 45 minutes
12 portion size

Ingredients:
1 tablespoon basil
1 tsp nutmeg
1 teaspoon black pepper
1 tablespoon of Italian seasoning
2 celery stalks
12 oz. tomato paste
1 14 oz. can tiny tomatoes
2 small shredded carrots
34 cup red wine, dry
1 34th cup water
1 pound of delicious Italian sausage
1 onion
3 garlic cloves

1 big breast of chicken
Cheese Stuffing
14 cup parsley, chopped
1-quart parmesan cheese
2 cups shredded mozzarella
Sauce Blanche
12 cup half & half
1/12 cup milk
1 teaspoon sea salt
1 teaspoon nutmeg
14 cup all-purpose flour
14 cup softened butter

Method:
1. Preheat the oven to 350 degrees
Fahrenheit.
2. Prepare your meat sauces.
3. Heat the bacon, ham, and onion
separately.
4. Combine the wine, tomato sauce, and
water in a small saucepan.
5. The remaining components are added.
Incorporate the bacon and chicken.
6. Bring to a boil and leave to cook for an
hour.
7. Set aside the parsley, grated cheese,
and Mozzarella in separate bowls.
8. Keep the sauce clear at all times. Melt
the butter in a small saucepan over medium
heat.

9. Mix in the flour thoroughly. Put in the cream, half and half, and nutmeg.
10. Continue to stir while boiling until the sauce turns viscous, similar to sour cream. Remove from the heat.
11. Spread 1 cup of meat sauce over the bottom of a 13x9-inch baking dish.
12. Top with as many lasagne noodles as desired.
13. Spread half of the white liquid over the noodles.
14. Spread a quarter of the Mozzarella mixture over the white sauce.
15th layer: lasagne noodles, meat sauce, and mixed mozzarella.
Then comes the mozzarella mixture, lasagne, white sauce, and meat sauce.
17. Bake at 350° for 45 minutes or until done.

Valtellina Pizzoccheri (Valtellina Pizzoccheri)

1 hour of cooking time
Size of each serving: 4

Ingredients:
grana Padano cheese, grated
Salt
3/4 cup 00 Italian flour
6 garlic cloves

10.5 ounces potatoes
2 1/2 sticks of butter
Casera cheese (7 oz.)
1/2 cup buckwheat flour
14 ounces savoy cabbage

Method:
1. Prepare the vegetables: peel them and cut them into semi-circles; cut and center the cabbage.
2. Cut the loaf in half and scrape out the ribs before slicing them into 1-inch thick slices.
3. In a skillet, toast the Italian 00 flour and buckwheat flour with a pinch of salt, then add 1 cup of flour and two tablespoons of water and begin kneading.
4. Turn the bread onto a floured board and rapidly stir with your palms until soft and flat.
5. In a large saucepan, combine 6 quarts of stock, the salt, and, once boiling, the cabbage; simmer for 10 minutes.
6. Return to a simmer and cook for another ten minutes. After that, add the potatoes.
7. Using a rolling pin, stretch the dough out from a 34-inch thick surface; slice it into 4-inch pieces, then horizontally cut each slice into half-inch broad portions.
8. Cut the garlic cloves in half and sauté in the oil until they are transparent.

9. Remove them from the oil. With the Casera butter, cut into cubes.
10. Add the pizzoccheri to the liquid with the veggies and boil for ten minutes.
11. Remove the pizzoccheri, potatoes, and vegetables from the water with a skimmer and place them on a tray.
12. Cover with sheets of cheese cubes, oil, and enough rubbed Grana Padano. Serve immediately.

Soup with Northern Beans and Vegetables

Time to cook: 35 minutes
Servings per recipe: 6
Ingredients:
parsley (fresh)
Parmesan cheese, grated
1 tablespoon extra virgin olive oil
3 canned white beans (15 oz.)
2 cups fresh baby spinach
1 tsp. kosher salt
12 tsp black pepper
1 medium onion
1 teaspoon thyme dried
½ teaspoon dried oregano
2 cloves garlic
1 rib celery
6 cups vegetable stock
1 medium carrot

Method:
1. Heat the olive oil over medium-high heat in a large saucepan or frying pan.
2. Place the onions in the oven for 5 minutes or until they are translucent.
3. Add the garlic, fennel, onions, thyme, oregano, salt, and black pepper and cook for another 2-3 minutes.
4. To incorporate the spices, add the vegetable stock and beans, bring to a simmer, reduce to low heat, and cook for fifteen minutes.
5. Stir in the spinach and cook for about two minutes or until the spinach defrosts.
6. Remove from the pan and immediately top with grated parmesan and fresh parsley, if desired.

2.3 Recipes for Dinner and Dessert

Stew with Veal from Northern Italy

Time to cook: 9 hours
Servings per recipe: 6

Ingredients:
3 cups orzo cooked
Grated lemon zest as a garnish
2 teaspoons rosemary, fresh
1 tomato can, diced
¼ cup shallots, chopped

one bay leaf
¾ cup chicken broth
1 ½ cup carrots, chopped
¾ cup celery, diced
1 ½ pound veal shoulder
¼ cup all-purpose flour

Method:
1. Combine the broth, vinegar, and flour in a 3/12-quarter or larger slow cooker.
2. Stir in the remaining ingredients, excluding the orzo.
3. Cover and bake for 7 to 9 hours or until the veal is juicy.
Spray with lime juice and parsley. Serve with orzo.

Pasta with Asparagus from Northern Italy

1 hour of cooking time
Size of each serving: 4

Ingredients:
to flavor with black pepper
4 tbsp olive oil (extra virgin)
320g fusilli
50g Parmigiano-Reggiano
salt
1 or 2 zucchini
Robiola cheese, 200 g
400g green asparagus, fresh

1-2 cloves garlic
1 bunch of fresh parsley
1 onion

Method:
1. Cut the onion and garlic into thin slices, then finely slice the onion.
2. Clean the asparagus, then break off the complex piece of the stalks.
3. Cut the parsley into little cubes and combine it with the zucchini.
4. Heat the oil in a large saucepan or skillet large enough to hold the noodles and sauces later, then add the garlic and onions and stir for 5 minutes.
5. Transfer the zucchini slices to the garlic and onion with a tablespoon of water and a pinch of salt, blend, and then simmer for ten minutes over a low burner.
6. Meanwhile, blanch the asparagus in salted water for about ten minutes.
7. Wash them after cooking, but keep the hot water in which the pasta was cooked.
8. Cut the asparagus in half and hold the spears back.
9. Mix the asparagus stalk and a little water in a mixing bowl or mixer. Place the mixed asparagus in a cup.
Then combine the zucchini, garlic, and onion mixture.

11. Combine the two sauces and return the sauce to the deep fryer.
12. Add the robiola, some Parmigiano, and most parsley.
13. Cook, stirring constantly, until the robiola has dissolved.
14. Season with salt, black pepper, and some asparagus stems to taste.
15. You may make the sauce fluffier after baking the pasta by adding a few teaspoons more spaghetti braising liquid.
16. If necessary, add a little water to the boiling water for the asparagus.
17. Cook the noodles in this bath until they are al dente, according to the package directions.
18. Wash the pasta and add it to the asparagus mixture.
19. Serve with the remaining asparagus leaves, extra shredded cheese, black pepper, and a sprinkling of coriander leave to combine the pasta and sauce thoroughly.

Stuffed Northern Italian Shells

1 hour 15 minutes to cook
Size of each serving: 15

Ingredients:
Spaghetti sauce, 32 oz. Rinaldi, Francesco
2 large eggs

2 (16-ounce) pasta shells Jumbo Barilla
pasta
1 teaspoon sea salt
½ teaspoon black pepper
10 oz. 3 packages of frozen spinach
2 medium onions
Sargentos Parmesan cheese, 8 oz.
3-pound ground round
2 8-oz. packets of Philadelphia cream
cheese

Method:
1. Place spinach in a ramekin and run under
warm water until defrosted.
2. Squeeze out the water and place it in a
large dish. Simply set it aside.
3. In a large sauté skillet, heat the
ground rounded till golden brown.
4. Drain the steak, then return it to the
pan with the fat.
5. Whip the cream cheese with an electric
mixer once it's all incorporated.
6. Evenly distribute the spinach, then add
the eggs, spice, peppers, and spinach to
the blender and blend again.
7. Add beef to the spinach mixture.
8. In the remaining meat fat, sauté the
sliced onions until tender, about 5
minutes.
9. Add the other ingredients to the bowl
with the vegetables.

10. Stir in the grated parmesan cheese to combine the ingredients.
11. Preheat the microwave to 350°F.
12. Cook the pasta cores in salted water until al dente, about ten minutes. If you overheat the shells, they will disintegrate.
13. Soak the shells on waxed paper to cold and clean them further.
14. Fill the shells with the beef/spinach mixture.
15. Coat two 9x13' glass baking plates with sunflower oil and melted butter.
16. Place shells in basins and cover them with plastic wrap. Top with pasta sauce. Layer the remaining shells on top of the gravy.
17. Repeat the layering of the shells with the additional spaghetti sauce. Wrap in foil and bake for approximately 1 hour.
18. Top the shells with more parmesan cheese and, if desired, fresh, ripped parsley.

Bonet: Northern Italian Baked Custard Dessert

1 hour 10 minutes to cook
Size of servings: 4-6

Ingredients:
Caramel
80g of water
125g of sugar
To make Custard
1/4 cup coffee
10g liqueur amaretto
100g of sugar
25g cocoa (dark)
30 grams of dark chocolate
4 eggs
250g milk
Amoretti cookies (50g)

Method:
1. Arrange six ramekins on the countertop.
2. In a small saucepan, combine water and sugar and stir well before the mixture becomes molten; heat over medium heat and simmer until the glucose is dissolved, resulting in a light golden sauce.
3. Remove from the heat and pour the caramel evenly over the bottom of the ramekins; set aside to cool while the custard is made.
4. Preheat the oven to 350°F.
5. Mash the Amoretti in a blender or food processor.
6. Melt the dairy and milk chocolate in a big saucepan.

7. While the milk is sweetening, combine the eggs and sugars in a small cup.
8. Stream and thoroughly mix the hot milk.
9. Combine the biscuits with the ground amoretti, sifted sugar, coffee, and amaretto liqueur, and mix well.
10. Spoon the mixture into the caramel-filled ramekins and create a bain-marie by placing the ramekins in a small dish.
11. Bake for about thirty minutes, or until the custard is set in the bottom area of the oven, covered with heated water halfway up the ramekins' borders.
12. Allow it to cool completely and for at least four hours before serving on a tray.
13. Soak the mold in warm water for 20 minutes to serve.
14. Trim the edges with a paring knife and alter the bonnet on the serving tray.

Recipes from Central Italy, Chapter 3

3.1 Recipes for Appetizers and Breakfast

Fried Rice Balls from Central Italy

Time to cook: 10 minutes
Size of each serving: 8

Ingredients:
For frying, use oil.
Dip in marinara sauce
2 tbsp. parmesan cheese
1 egg
4 cups cold risotto
1 cup bread crumbs (panko)
8 balls of mozzarella

Method:
1. Begin by dividing your risotto into equal portions.
2. Roll each risotto quarter into a large ball.
3. Place a mozzarella ball in the center of each Arancini.
4. Use your fingers to mold the risotto into a circular shape.

5. Arrange each arancini ball on a baking sheet lined with parchment paper and sprayed with oil.
Allow it to freeze for ten minutes.
6. Combine the panko breadcrumbs and the sliced parmesan in a mixing bowl.
7. Crack an egg into a small container.
8. Remove the arancini from the refrigerator, roll each one in the egg, then roll in the panko bread crumbs.
9. Heat the oil in a large saucepan or frying pan until it reaches 350 degrees.
10. Cook the arancini until golden brown on the outside, flipping to cook both sides evenly.
11. Wipe with a clean cloth-lined plate. Serve with sour cream to dip.

Toasted Garlic Bread from Central Italy

Time to cook: 15 minutes
Servings per container: 10

Ingredients:
seasoned with salt & pepper
1 cup shredded mozzarella
3 garlic cloves
1 teaspoon dried oregano
1 loaf (1 pound) of Italian bread
2 tsp extra virgin olive oil
5 teaspoons melted butter

Method:
1. Preheat the oven to 350°F.
2. Cut the bread into 2-inch thick slices.
3. Combine the sugar, olive oil, cloves, oregano, salt, and black pepper in a shallow dish.
4. Evenly sprinkle the mixture on the bread slices.
5. Arrange the slices evenly on a large baking sheet and broil for 5 minutes or until gently browned.
6. Check them frequently to avoid burning them.
7. Remove from the oven.
8. Return to the oven for 3 minutes or until the cheese is finely browned and melted. Serve immediately.

Central Italian Rice Stuffed Tomatoes

1 hour 20 minutes to cook
Size of each serving: 5

Ingredients:
1/4 to 1/2 cups tomato pulp
2 to 3 tbsp olive oil
6 Italian parsley sprigs
1 sliced garlic clove
4 to 5 tomatoes
1 tablespoon basil

½ teaspoon of salt
1 teaspoon dried oregano
1 cup uncooked rice (185 g)

Method:
1. Preheat the oven to 375°F before heating the oil in a large mixing bowl.
2. Place the rice in a small basin, cover it with water, and set aside for 1 hour before rinsing and draining.
3. Wash and clean the tomatoes, then chop off a piece and lay it aside.
4. Separate the veggies from the seed and pulp, reserving the pulp and discarding the seeds.
5. Mix the diced tomato paste, oregano, cinnamon, parsley, cloves, 2-3 tablespoons olive oil, and rice in a medium mixing bowl.
Cover the mixture with the hollowed-out tomato. Replace the tops of the tomatoes, sprinkle with salt, and drizzle with olive oil.
7. Sprinkle the rosemary over the roasted potatoes and bake for 45-50 minutes, or until the potatoes and rice are tender. Instantly serve.

Central Italian Risotto with Pumpkin and Red Radicchio

1 hour 20 minutes to cook
Size of each serving: 4

Ingredients:
season with pepper to taste
Season with salt to taste
Vinegar of red wine
a little rosemary
1 tiny red radicchio head
a little veggie broth
EVOO (extra virgin olive oil)
1 gram sheet of gelatin
1 scallion
1 lupin
Cream, whipped
2 ounces squash

Method:
1. For less than two minutes, caramelize
the radicchio ends in unsalted hot water.
2. Drain and rinse the leaves with cloths.
3. Combine the vinegar, 14 cup of the oil,
and two tablespoons of salt in a mixing
bowl, and add the still-warm radicchio
leaf.
4. Caramelize for 6 hours. Drain and
carefully chop the radicchio.
5. Clean the gelatin layer with a small
amount of water.
6. Bake the squash for about thirty minutes
at 350°F.

7. Pass the squash through a sieve, then immediately insert the saturated and squeezed-out gelatin, allowing it to breakdown with the squash's remaining heat.
8. Season the whipped cream with pepper and salt.
9. Pour the mixture over four bubble wrap sheets and pack them together, wrapping the flaps completely to seal them.
10. Refrigerate them for at least three hours.
11. Remove them from the fridge, carefully cut the plastic wrap, and set aside for at least 20 minutes until the dish is done.
12. Wash the lentils for a few minutes in cold water.
13. Saute the shallot in a little oil for two minutes, then add the washed lentils, a sprig of thyme, and a ladle of soup; bring to a boil, then reduce to a low heat and stew for around thirty minutes. To taste, season with salt.
14. Blend until your pâté becomes a smooth sauce.
15. Layer the soft lentil pâté in the baking pans, followed by the radicchio and baby pumpkins.
16. Decorate with pumpkin seeds whichever you choose.

Arugula and Central Italian Barbecue Steak

Time to cook: 28 minutes
Servings per recipe: 2

Ingredients:
2 tomatoes, cut into wedges
The Parmigiano Reggiano chunk
6 oz. arugula
½ lemon juice
1lb boneless strip steak
a pinch of sea salt
ground black pepper, freshly ground
Olive oil, extra virgin

Method:
1. Brush both ends of the steak with olive oil and season lightly with salt and black pepper. Allow it to cool to room temperature.
2. Light a fire in a fuel or barbecue grill.
3. Cook, turning once, until the big or medium-rare steak is cooked and baked.
4. Transfer to a chopping board with tweezers and leave for a few moments before draining the juices again.
5. In a large mixing bowl, combine the arugula with two tablespoons olive oil, lime juice to taste, and season with salt and pepper.

6. Divide the vegetables between two dinner plates.
7. Cut the meat against the grain on a diagonal and place it in the center of the greens.
8. Using a vegetable peeler, shave the Parmigiano peel, allowing the shavings to fall right into the salad.
9. Arrange tomato slices along the sides of the dishes.

3.2 Recipes for Snacks and Lunch

Pasta with Mushrooms and Peas from Central Italy

Time to cook: 50 minutes
Size of each serving: 4

Ingredients:
14 cup whipped cream
to taste, ground pepper
14 glass white wine
1 cup chicken stock
2 cups cremini quartered
1 tbsp. all-purpose flour
8 oz. whole wheat pasta
2 oz. prosciutto
2 garlic cloves
1 teaspoon olive oil (extra virgin)
3 cups peas, shelled

Method:

1. Bring a large saucepan of water to a boil.
2. Add the pasta and veggies; cook for 10-15 minutes, or until the pasta is soft and the peas are tender.
3. In the meantime, heat the oil in a large casserole dish over medium heat.
4. Cook the prosciutto for about 5 minutes, rotating once, until it begins to brown.
5. Stir in the garlic and cook for thirty seconds, or until fragrant.
6. Stir in the mushrooms for about four minutes, or until the juices are released and most of the liquid has evaporated.
7. Spray the mushrooms with flour and toss to coat. Allow the wine to boil for two minutes.
8. Stir in the broth and return to a boil for about three minutes, or until the sauce thickens.
9. Turn off the heat. Mix in the pepper and cream.
10. Wipe the peas and noodles clean; add the mushrooms sauce, transfer to a mixing dish, and toss to coat.

Spinach Risotto from Central Italy

2 hours to prepare

Size of each serving: 4

Ingredients:
50g Parmigiano-Reggiano
Pepper
Season with salt to taste
30 gram(s) butter
12 oz. white wine
1 liter of stock
rice 350 grams
½ onion
2 tbsp olive oil (extra virgin)
Spinach 400 grams

Method:
1. Begin by brushing and drying the spinach.
2. Caramelize them for 1 to 2 minutes in boiling, salted water, then remove them with a rubber spatula and immerse them in an ice bath or briefly under cold water to keep their dark green color.
3. To cook the rice, save the liquid from steaming the spinach and use it as stock.
4. After the spinach has completely cooled, mix it into a sauce using an immersion blender. Set it away.
5. Return the stock to the flames. When making risotto, the stock should be extremely hot so that the rice heat does not diminish when you add the liquid.

6. Place the cut onions and vegetable oil in a pan and cook over low heat until the onion turns smooth and translucent.
7. Stir in the rice and cook for 2 minutes, or until the rice is translucent.
8. Pour in the white wine and allow the liquor to burn off over a hot flame.
9. To fill the rice, add enough stock and reduce the heat to medium.
10. Continue stirring, frequently combining the rice and gradually adding stock until the rice is done.
11. Depending on the rice you use, it will take between 18 and 20 minutes to make.
12. Add the combined spinach about five minutes before the risotto is ready, mix thoroughly with the rice, and keep stirring.
13. If the rice is done, turn off the heat and add the oil and diced Parmigiano Reggiano. Combine thoroughly before it becomes creamy.
14 Please make sure your risotto is airy and not sticky.
You can do this by adding 1 or 2 teaspoons more stock if necessary.
15. Taste them for salt and pepper to your liking.
16. Garnish with a sprinkling of freshly ground black pepper and a little extra grated Parmigiano Reggiano on the edge.

Polenta Central Italiana with Pork Rib Sauce

2 hours to prepare
Servings per recipe: 6

Ingredients:
a quarter teaspoon of salt
1 ½ cup water
2 bay leaves
¼ cup of wine
Flakes of hot pepper
2 rosemary sprigs
1 pound ribs of pork
2 tbsp of olive oil
2 garlic cloves
½ cup pureed tomatoes
5 sausages from Italy

To make the Polenta
½ teaspoon of salt
7 quarts of water
2 cups flour (cornmeal)

Method:
1. In a large pot over medium heat, combine the butter, garlic, meat, rib, seasoning to taste, and a dash of pepper; cook the meat from both sides.

2. Add the bay leaf and rosemary, raise the temperature, and add the wine. Simmer until the wine has evaporated (about five minutes), then add the tomato sauce and water, and stir to combine.
3. Bring to a boil, then reduce to a simmer for about 1 hour, or until the meat is tender. Salt it to taste.
4. Make the Polenta while the sauce is heating up.
5. Bring the water to a boil in a large pot, then gradually add the cornmeal.
6. Whisk continually to combine; after it begins to boil, lower heat but continue to stir often; cook whisking for 45-50 minutes, or until heavy.
7. Season with salt to taste. Serve immediately with sauces and a heavy covering of freshly grated Parmesan.

3.3 Recipes for Dinner and Dessert

Central Italian Chicken Cacciatore

Time to cook: 6 hours
Size of servings: 4-6

Ingredients:
2 tbsp. Worcestershire sauce
seasoned with salt & pepper
shredded chicken

1 tbsp each fresh basil and oregano
1/2 cup sliced black olives
1/2 cup of red wine
1/2 liters chicken broth
2 cans chopped tomatoes
1/4 cup tomato puree
1 medium onion
1 teaspoon garlic
four tiny potatoes
8 little button mushrooms

Method:
1. Brown chicken chunks in a frying pan.
2. Cut the mushrooms, tomatoes, and potatoes into small pieces.
3. Arrange the chicken and vegetables in the bottom of the dish.
4. Spill everything else around the corner.
5. Swirl it through to bring it through. Cook for 6-7 hours, or until the chicken is done.
7. If the sauce is excessively watery, moisten it with cornflour mixed with a liquid for about thirty minutes before serving.
8. Serve with cheesy polenta or spaghetti.

Central Italian Pork Cutlet with Balsamic Vinegar

1 hour 25 minutes to cook

Size of each serving: 5

Ingredients:
1 tsp. kosher salt
1/2 teaspoon black pepper
1 teaspoon garlic
2 tsp. fresh rosemary
four to five boneless pork chops
two tbsp balsamic vinegar
1/4 cup extra virgin olive oil

Method:
1. Whisk together the olive oil, balsamic vinegar, ginger, thyme, salt, and black pepper in a cup.
2. Dip the pork chops in the marinade, covering both ends.
3. Place the pork chops in a small dish or a thick plastic bag with a tight fitting lid.
4. Pour the remaining marinade over the pork chops.
5. Wrap the bag or cover the bowl in plastic wrap and place in the refrigerator for 1-2 hours.
6. Grill the pork chops for four minutes per side, or until they reach 145°.
7. Preheat the oven to 375°F for baking.
8. Bake for 10 minutes, then flip the pork chops.

9. Bake for ten minutes, or until completely cooked.
10. Serve immediately.

Milanese Stewed Beef Shanks from Central Italy

Time to cook: 5 hours 15 minutes
Size of each serving: 4

Ingredients:
½ cup beef broth
Season with salt and pepper to taste.
½ cup white wine, dry
one 540 mL can of tomatoes
½ medium white onion
2 carrots (medium)
2 to 3 pound beef shanks
2 teaspoons garlic mince
¼ cup melted butter

Method:
1. If desired, wash and coat the meat chunks with flour.
2. Heat the oil in a large ovensafe beef stock pan over medium-high heat.
3. Fry the beef shanks in the fat until golden brown on the outside.
4. Place the beef shanks in a pan and keep heated.

5. Add the onion slices to the pan and cook until the onion is tender.
6. Add the garlic and carrots and simmer until the garlic is fragrant.
7. Pour in the white wine and sauté the pan at this point.
8. Combine the beef with the liquid and tomatoes.
9. Return the beef to the pan, making sure the sauce is completely submerged in the shanks.
10. Put the lid on the edge and roast the shanks for five hours at 300°F, or until the flesh is cooked and the bone falls off.
11. Cover and simmer for three hours on the stovetop over medium heat.
12. Inspect and rotate the meat on a regular basis to ensure that the bottom is not browned.

Panettone Central Italian Stuffed

Time to cook: 50 minutes
Size of each serving: 4

Ingredients:
a couple of frozen dark cherries
Brush the sides with liqueur
1 pound panettone
1 vanilla

1 chocolate
2 quarts of gelato

Method:
1. Turn the panettone horizontally and cut
an inch from the bottom, or make the
incision under the dome on the upper right.
2. Take out a sharp serrated knife.
3. Then, cut it out along the inside,
leaving 12 inch of foundation and sides.
4. Fill the space tightly down to the top
with melted ice cream, then firmly re-
attach the lid or rim.
5. Wrap all of the panettones in foil or
plastic wrap and store in the refrigerator.
6. Remove from the refrigerator, unwrap,
and remove the foil from the panettone,
then place on a serving plate and decorate
the end.
7. Cut into pieces and serve.

Cookies with Almonds from Central Italy

1 hour 25 minutes to cook
Size of Servings: 24

Ingredients:
½ tsp baking powder
¼ cup confectioners' sugar
2 teaspoons honey
2 tbsp almond flour

1 quart granulated sugar
1 orange's zest
¼ cup beaten egg whites

Method:
1. In a large mixing bowl, whisk together the egg whites, butter, orange zest, and syrup until creamy.
2. Add the almond flour and baking soda and combine until wet. Dissolve all of the dry ingredients in the moist and mix with a spoon or soapy sponge.
3. Cover and chill for one hour to up to 24 hours.
4. Preheat the oven to 325°F while prepared to roast, with two racks in the top two positions.
5. Line two baking pans with parchment paper.
6. Place the powdered sugar in a small cup.
7. Roll the mixture into a fat log on your table with your fingertips and divide it into two equal sections.
8. Roll each piece into a log and cut it in half, then cut each half twice. Then cut each piece into three pieces.
9. Roll each chunk into a ball and roll in powdered sugar on the baking sheets, 12 per tray.
10. Cook both together for 15 minutes, flipping the plates halfway through.

11. The cookies are done when they start to crackle and straighten out and are lightly browned on the rim.
12. The cores will be sensitive, so don't go by the cookie's instincts and continue to leave the baking sheet on.
13. They have a crisp outside and a chewy inside and tighten up as they cool on the baking sheet.
14 Store it at room temperature in an airtight bag.

Recipes from Southern Italy, Chapter 4

Recipes for Appetizers and Breakfast

Toasts with garlic-ricotta and hot honey, and Southern Italian broccoli

Time to cook: 15 minutes
Size of each serving: 5

Ingredients:
1 1/2 cup ricotta fresh
The spice black pepper
3 cups pre-cooked broccoli
1 tablespoon vinegar (white wine)
1/2 tsp red pepper flakes
1 sliced baguette
Kosher salt is kosher salt.
1 teaspoon honey
Extra virgin olive oil

Method:
1. Preheat the oven to 350°F to bake the baguette slices.
2. Brush each slice with a little olive oil and place them on a baking sheet.
3. Bake for 12 minutes, or until lightly golden brown. Remove it from the oven to cool.
4. Whisk together the honey, vinegar, and pepper flakes in a small pan.
5. In a small bowl, whip the ricotta until creamy, then season with salt.
6. Spread the ricotta over the bread and top with the roasted vegetables.
7. Arrange a plate and glaze it correctly with a honey mixture.

Salad with Oregano-Marinated Tomatoes

Time to cook: 45 minutes
Size of servings: 4-6

Ingredients:
2 tsp. kosher salt
1 teaspoon ground black pepper
2 tbsp olive oil (extra virgin)
2 tbsp. oregano leaves
3 pound tomatoes

Method:
1. Combine the tomatoes, oil, oregano,
pepper, and spice in a large mixing bowl.
2. Leave it for at least thirty minutes and
up to an hour, flipping frequently, until
juicy and highly flavored.

**Sun-Dried Tomatoes, Artichoke Hearts, and
Pasta with Sausage**

Time to cook: 25 minutes
Size of each serving: 4

Ingredients:
ground black pepper, freshly ground
¼ cup bell pepperoncini
marinated artichoke hearts (24 oz.)

sun-dried tomatoes ¾ cup
1 lb. spaghetti
4 ounces dry-cured ham
two tbsp tomato paste
Kosher salt is kosher salt.
2 tbsp extra virgin olive oil
1/4 cup pine nuts

Method:
1. Cook the pasta in a large pot of boiling salted water, stirring occasionally, until al dente.
2. Drain the pasta and reserve 1 cup of the cooking liquid; return the spaghetti to the saucepan.
3. Toast the pine nuts in a small empty skillet over medium-high heat, stirring frequently, for 3-5 minutes or until beautifully toasted.
Transfer it to a small container.
4. Heat the oil in a large skillet over medium-high heat.
5. Stir in the tomato sauce and bacon for two minutes.
6. Cook for about two minutes, stirring constantly, until the artichokes and sun-dried tomato are well cooked. Remove from the heat.
7. Combine the sausage mixture and ¾ cup of pasta cooking liquid in a pasta dish; spritz with ¼ teaspoon chile.

8. Flip to coat and use the remaining ¼ cup pasta cooking liquid to lose if necessary.
9. Separate the spaghetti into pans. On the edge, sprinkle with pepper seasoning and pepperoncini.

Pasta Primavera in One Pot with Shrimp from Southern Italy

Time to cook: 22 minutes
Size of each serving: 4

Ingredients:
¼ cups basil
Flakes of red pepper
12 oz. short pasta
1 tsp. lemon zest
¾ cup Parmesan cheese
1 frozen cup green peas
3 tbsp unsweetened butter
8 oz. big shrimp
1-quart cherry tomatoes
4 cloves garlic
1 bag (10 oz.) frozen broccoli florets
6 oz. green beans
¾ tsp black pepper
2 ½ kosher salt teaspoons

Method:

1. Place the spaghetti in a large, flat-bottomed pot or large, flat, directly plate.
2. Add the garlic, black pepper, lime juice, and 3½ cups of heated water.
3. Bring them to a boil, covered.
4. Once heated, unfold and cook the pasta according to the package directions and toss frequently.
5. Stir in the broccoli and green beans when the timer goes off for five minutes.
6. Replace the lid on the saucepan and bring it back to a boil.
7. After two minutes, stir in the seafood, onions, peas, and butter.
8. Cook for two minutes with the lid closed, then open and cook for another minute, mixing constantly, until the pasta is soft, the seafood is thoroughly cooked, and the water nearly evaporates.
9. Remove from the heat. Swirl in ¾ cup of Parmesan and lemon zest to cover. If desired, season with additional salt and black pepper.
10. Separate the pasta into pans. Finish with basil, more Parmesan cheese, and bell pepper, if using.

Crudo of Sea Bream with Lemon and Olives

1 hour of cooking time

Size of each serving: 8

Ingredients:
EVOO (extra virgin olive oil)
Sea salt flaky
2 ripe plum tomatoes
½ medium red onion
½ cup freshly squeezed lemon juice
Kosher salt is kosher salt.
½ lemon
1 pound arugula
¼ cup olives Niçoise
12 pound sea bream

Method:
1. Grate tomatoes on a grater until all the material is chopped, and the skin is removed; discard the skin.
2. Place the tomato paste in a shallow pot and season with kosher salt.
3. Cut half the lime into quarters and remove the seeds and white rind. Cut the pieces into quarters.
4. Slide the fish onto the panel.
5. Holding a large knife at a 45° angle, cut the flesh into 14'-thick pieces with the grains (use a sharp edge and a broad, straight stroke).
6. Cut each piece lengthwise in half.
7. Arrange sea bream on cold plates.

8. Spoon a little grated tomato around and top with lemon slices.
9. Arrange arugula, olives, and onions on top.
10. Drizzle with lime juice, then drizzle with oil and season with sea salt.

Recipes for Snacks and Lunch

Salad with Tomatoes and Mozzarella

Time to cook: 15 minutes
Size of servings: 4-6

Ingredients:
4 tbsp balsamic vinegar
salt that is kosher
1/2 cup ripped basil leaves
three tbsp olive oil
1/2 pound fresh mozzarella cheese
three tomatoes

Method:
1. Cut the mozzarella and tomato into large chunks.
2. Pour the olive oil and vinegar over the basil leaves.
3. Give it a little stir.
4. Spray it with a bit of spice.
5. Relax for at least an hour.

6. Refrigerate or store in a fabulous location.

Spring Risotto from Southern Italy

1 hour of cooking time
Servings per recipe: 6

Ingredients:
1 frozen cup peas
½ cup grated Parmesan cheese
1 pound Arborio rice
½ cup dry white wine
2 cans sodium-free chicken broth
black pepper
½ cup onions
1 to 2 medium zucchini
salt, coarse
3 teaspoons melted butter

Method:
1. Heat the broth and 212 cups of water in a small saucepan over medium heat; keep heated.
2. In the meantime, melt two tablespoons of butter in a 3-quarter saucepan over medium heat.
3. Add the zucchini and season with salt and pepper. Cook, stirring occasionally, for 10 minutes or until the zucchini is transparent.

4. Using a rubber spatula, transfer the zucchini to a platter.
5. Reduce the heat to medium-low. Cook for 5 minutes or until the onion is soft.
6. Season with 1 teaspoon salt and 14 teaspoon pepper.
Reduce the heat.
7. Add rice and mix for four minutes or until the sides are transparent.
8. Pour the wine and let it soak for about two minutes.
9. Cook for 25 minutes, adding 1 cup of hot liquid at a time (stir until nearly all of the liquid has been drained before adding more), until the rice is tender.
10. Add the zucchini and peas and cook for two minutes until the peas are light green.
11. Remove from the heat. Add the parmesan cheese and the remaining tablespoon of butter. Eat after finishing with more cheese.

Southern Italian Escarole with Italian Sausage and White Beans

1 hour 10 minutes to cook
12 portion size

Ingredients:
1 cup chicken broth
Parmigiano-Reggiano cheese

¾ cup white wine, dry
4 cans (15 oz.) Great Northern beans
three tbsp olive oil
½ tsp red pepper
1 huge escarole head
½ c. prosciutto
1 teaspoon garlic
12 sausages from Italy
1 onion cup

Method:
1. Heat the oil in a large, heated pan over medium-high heat.
2. Working in batches, sauté sausage once cooked over, a rupture with a spoon back, approximately six minutes every load.
3. Using a slotted spoon, transfer the sausage to the bowl, leaving the drippings in the saucepan.
4. Reduce heat to low; add onion to skillet and sauté for 5 minutes or until translucent.
5. Garnish with prosciutto and cook for another two minutes.
6. Add the garlic and smashed red pepper to the mixture.
7. Add the escarole and cook for about two minutes, or until softened. Simmer for two minutes after adding the wine.
8. To combine tastes, cook rice, stocks, and sausage for 10 minutes.

9. Season with salt and pepper to taste. Transfer it to a large bowl. If desired, top with grated Parmesan.

Chicken in a Single Skillet with Buttery Orzo

2 hours to prepare
Size of each serving: 4

Ingredients:
1 tablespoon freshly squeezed lemon juice
1 tsp. lemon zest
Kosher salt is kosher salt.
¼ cup white wine, dry
2 ½ cup chicken broth (low sodium)
black pepper
1 leek
8 oz of orzo
6 chicken thighs, bone-in
1 bulb fennel
3 tbsp unsweetened butter

Method:
1. Preheat the oven to 400° F.
2. Season the meat liberally with salt and black pepper. 2 tbsp butter, on a medium-high pan.
3. Place the chicken, skin side down, in a thin layer in the skillet with no holes.

4. Cook for 6-8 minutes until the flesh is transparent around the edges and the skin is richly browned.
5. Place the skillet in the oven, skin side up, and bake for 10 minutes, or until the chicken is fried.
Place your chicken in a dish.
6. Heat the same pan over medium heat; combine the fennel bulb and leek in a skillet and season with salt and pepper.
7. Cook for about five minutes, flipping frequently, until the leek is golden on the exterior.
8. Add orzo and cook for three minutes until the pasta has faded to a light nutty color with a toasted aroma.
9. Pour in the wine and heat for about two minutes or until the liquid has evaporated.
10. Add half a cup of soup at a time, stirring constantly and letting the stock soak before adding more until the orzo is soft and most of the broth has been drunk.
11. Remove the skillet from the oven, season with salt and black pepper to taste, and combine with the remaining two tablespoons of lemon juice.
12. Arrange the fennel, butter, and lemon zest on the chicken.

Pasta e Fagioli with Escarole from Southern Italy

1 hour 40 minutes to cook
Size of each serving: 4

Ingredients:
3 oz. dried lasagna
12 tiny head escarole
1 can (14.5 oz.) tomatoes
¾ cup white wine, dry
Cannellini beans, 1½ cups
three tbsp olive oil
1 medium onion
1 rind of Parmesan
Kosher salt is kosher salt.
black pepper
2 carrots (medium)
two bay leaves
2 chiles de árbol dried
6 parsley sprigs
1 rosemary sprig
2 stalks celery
1 garlic head

Method:
1. Bring the beans, carrots, Parmesan rind, fennel, garlic head, shallots, thyme, bay leaf, chiles, and two-quarters of the water to a boil in a medium bowl.
2. Reduce the heat to low and cover the pot until the beans are tender, about 112 hours.

3. Season with salt and pepper, remove from fire, and set aside for thirty minutes.
4. Discard some vegetables, rind, and seasonings.
5. In a large, medium pot, heat 3 tablespoons of oil.
6. Cook the onion and garlic powder for 8-10 minutes, stirring frequently, until soft.
7. Add the tomatoes, smash with your palms, and cook for 12 to 15 minutes, stirring regularly, until the liquid is nearly totally reduced.
8. Pour in the wine, bring to a boil, and cook for about five minutes, or until almost completely evaporated.
9. Add the beans and their liquid; simmer for 12 to 15 minutes, or until the flavors dissolve.
10. Add noodles and cook for 20 minutes, stirring occasionally and adding more hot water as needed, until al dente.
11. Add the escarole and heat for about 1 minute, or until softened; season with salt and pepper.
12. Show your support with an oil-drizzled broth topped with Pesto and more chiles.

Lemon and tomato-flavored fish

Time to cook: 20 minutes

Servings per recipe: 2

Ingredients:
2 fillets of whitefish
½ lemon slices
a handful of basil
1 bag (about 100g) spinach
1 garlic clove
400g chopped tomatoes
Fry with olive oil

Method:
1. Cook the cloves in a frying pan with 1 teaspoon olive oil for about thirty seconds, or until moist.
2. To moisten somewhat, add the tomatoes and aggressively bubble for about five minutes.
3. Season with basil and spinach. Place the cutlets on top, followed by a few lemon slices on each fillet.
4. Place in a small oven dish. Cook well, then grill for five minutes, or until the salmon is grilled through and transparent.
5. Serve with steamed lettuce or fresh potatoes.

4.3 Recipes for Dinner and Dessert

Amarone Risotto with Caramelized Radicchio

Time to cook: 45 minutes
Size of serving: 6-8

Ingredients:
6 cup chicken stock
1 cup grated Parmesan cheese
Arborio rice, 2 cups
1 quart Amarone
4 tbsp. melted butter
1 onion cup
2 big radicchio heads
¼ cup virgin olive oil

Method:
1. Melt one tablespoon of butter and one tablespoon of canola oil in a large, deep pot over medium heat.
2. Cook until the radicchio and onion are yellow, about eighteen minutes. Simply add rice.
3. Spray with pepper and salt; stir until the rice is translucent around the edges but opaque in the center for about four minutes.
4. Add the wine and simmer for about three minutes, or until the wine is gone, stirring occasionally.
5. Pour in 5 ½ cups broth, bring to a boil, and turn up the heat.
6. Simmer for about eight minutes, or until the rice is tender and the risotto is

smooth, stirring occasionally and adding
more soup as needed.
7. Remove the risotto from the heat and
stir in the remaining two tablespoons of
butter and grated parmesan. Season the
risotto with salt and pepper to taste.

Pasta with Herbs, Garlic, and Green Olives

Time to cook: 50 minutes
Size of each serving: 4

Ingredients:
1 cup fresh basil leaves
2 tsp. lemon juice
¼ tsp red pepper flakes
3 tbsp. unsalted butter
1 cup fresh parsley
1 cup olives Castelvetrano
pappardelle 12 oz.
¼ cup virgin olive oil
8 cloves garlic
Kosher salt is kosher salt.

Method:
1. Cook the pasta in a large pot of boiling
salted water, turning occasionally, until
al dente, about two minutes less than the
box guidelines.
2. Heat ¼ cup oil in a large Dutch oven or
other large pot over medium-high heat.

3. Add the chopped garlic and cook for about five minutes, stirring frequently and pressing down on the garlic to make a good touch with the pot's bottom.
4. Add the parsley and cook for about five minutes, stirring frequently, until it releases some of its moisture and blackens somewhat in color.
5. Stir in the olive and red pepper flakes and cook for another minute to combine the flavors.
6. Using tongs, transfer the pasta to a pot with the sauce and add the butter and ½ cup of the pasta boiling liquid.
7. Cook, swirling and adding additional liquid pasta as needed, until each spaghetti string is covered and the pasta is al dente, about three minutes.
8. Remove the pasta from the heat and stir in the basil, lime juice, and lemon zest. Taste and season with salt if necessary.
9. Divide the spaghetti into dishes and drizzle with additional oil.

Crostatas with Grapefruit and Orange from Southern Italy

2 hours 10 minutes to cook
Size of each serving: 4

Ingredients:

Dough
1 tsp. kosher salt
¼ tsp distilled white vinegar
a teaspoon of sugar
1 ¼ cup all-purpose flour
3/4 pound unsalted butter
Assembly and Frangipane
1 big egg
1 big yolk of an egg
¾ teaspoon vanilla extract or paste
4 tbsp. unsalted butter
1 pomegranate
one orange
½ cup spelled flour
1 tsp. kosher salt
4 ½ tsp all-purpose flour
7 teaspoon sugar

Method:
1. Using a whisk attachment, whisk together
the oil, flour, salt, and sugar until the
butter is nickel-sized or smaller in flat
sections.
2. In a small basin, combine the vinegar
and ¼ cup of ice water and whisk together
on low speed. Add another 1-2 teaspoons and
beat again.
3. Add ice water as needed until no dried
patches remain. Continue hammering until
the dough begins to clump together, but
stop when a ball begins to form.

4. Place the dough on a surface and pinch and flatten it a few times to pull it together.
5. Separate it into four sections. Flatten into 12-inch-thick disks and wrap in plastic. Chill for at least four hours and up to two days.
6. Preheat the oven to 400°F and position a shelf in the center.
7. Stir in the Semolina flour mixture, cinnamon, five teaspoons, and sugar. Add all-purpose flour to a medium mixing bowl.
8. In a separate small dish, coarsely grate the grapefruit and orange zest; set it aside with the fruit. Include the vanilla paste.
9. At room temperature, add the butter and zest and mix until smooth. Add the egg and egg yolk and vigorously stir to combine.
10. Add dry ingredients and mix only until combined.
Remove and discard the reserved citrus peel and rind.
11. Cut the fruit into thick 12-inch slices and wiggle the seeds out. Roll out 8 circles of dough on a lightly floured board, one at a time.
12 Spread 14 cup frangipane in the center of each on a parchment-lined sheet pan, making a 112-inch border.

13. Arrange orange rings on a baking sheet to cover with frangipane, then wrap the dough edges up and over the fruit. Chill for thirty minutes.

14. Brush the fruit and coating with the melting butter and sprinkle with the remaining two teaspoons of sugar.

15. Bake crostatas, flipping once, for 40-50 minutes, or until crusts are well browned with a few lighter places. Allow 10 minutes before serving to chill.

Leg of Lamb from Southern Italy with Garlic and Rosemary

Time to cook: 4 hours 15 minutes
12 portion size

Ingredients:
Extra virgin olive oil
Roasting bag, large
Garlic granules
2 c. Pinot Grigio wine
1 lamb leg weighing 5 lbs.
1 teaspoon dried oregano
parsley (fresh)
2 or 3 basil leaves, fresh
Season with salt and pepper to taste.
Mint leaves, fresh
a rosemary sprig
5 garlic cloves, fresh

Method:

1. Rub the lamb with sunflower oil.
2. Place the roasting bags or a large pan in a bread oven that has been sealed to match the leg.
3. Cut slits in the lamb's left and right sides and scatter entire garlic cloves around the lamb.
4. Evenly sprinkle with oregano and granulated cloves.
5. Sprinkle with fresh herbs.
6. Season with salt and pepper to taste.
7. Pour the wine down the bottom without reaching the meat, then add the limes if used on the top, sides, and underneath the lamb.
8. Close the bag or place the lid on the saucepan at midnight and marinate.
9. Preheat the oven to 425°F and then reduce it to 325°F.
10. Don't hold back on the liquids.
11. Roast at 325°F on the stove until a meat thermometer is used to prepare it.
12. A four to five-pound roast is usually ready in four hours.

Manicotti with Four Cheeses from Southern Italy

1 hour 40 minutes to cook

Servings per recipe: 6

Ingredients:
8 oz. mozzarella
1 scallions
6 tbsp unsweetened butter
¾ cup Pecorino Romano, grated
2 quarts whole milk
1 cup parmesan cheese, grated
1 pound freshly made ricotta
¼ cup regular flour
1 big egg
1 large onion
8 oz. manicotti noodle
Vegetable or olive oil
2 cloves garlic
1 can (14 oz.) tomatoes
¼ cup basil leaf
2 tbsp. kosher salt
1 can (28 oz.) tomatoes
¾ tsp ground pepper

Method:
1. Preheat the oven to 400° F.
2. Melt 2 tablespoons butter in a saucepan.
3. Heat a large skillet over medium heat.
Cook, stirring regularly, until the onion
and garlic are soft, about three minutes.
Season with 1 teaspoon each of salt and
pepper.

4. Add all tomato cans, divide with a wooden spoon, and turn the heat up to medium-high.
5. Add half a cup of basil, bring to a boil, and simmer for 20 minutes, stirring occasionally, until much reduced.
6. Cook the noodles until al dente in a large saucepan of boiling salted water, stirring often.
7. Drain and transfer to a well-oiled rimmed baking sheet.
8. Melt the remaining four tablespoons of butter in the meantime.
9. Stir in the flour and heat for 1-2 minutes, until it smells frothy and delicious.
10. While whisking continuously, gradually add milk and bring to a simmer.
11. Cook for about three minutes, stirring regularly, until the paste coats the back of a spoon.
12. Combine ¼ cup Parmesan cheese and ¼ cup Pecorino; season with half a teaspoon salt and the remaining 14 teaspoon chile.
13. In a medium mixing bowl, combine the ricotta, shallot, cheese, 14 cup Parmesan cheese, half a cup basil, twice a cup Pecorino, and 12 teaspoon salt.
14. Spoon the ricotta mixture on both sides of the manicotti pasta.

15. Spread half of the spaghetti sauce and half of the white sauce on the bottom of the baking dish. Layer the manicotti on top, then top with the remaining spaghetti sauce, cheese sauce, and 14 cup Parmesan.
16. Bake the manicotti for 30-40 minutes, or until the top is fizzy and lightly browned.
17. Allow for a five-minute cooling period. Top with the remaining 14 cup of basil and serve.

Casino Clams with Bacon and Bell Pepper

Time to cook: 25 minutes
Servings per recipe: 6

Ingredients:
2 tbsp fresh parsley
2 dozen small neck clams
a ¼ cup panko
three tbsp olive oil
4 bacon slices
1-2 cups kosher salt, coarse
2 teaspoons vinegar (white wine)
1 little red bell pepper
2 shallots, medium

Method:
1. Arrange a rack in the center of the oven and preheat to 500°F.

2. Cook bacon in a medium saucepan over medium-high heat, flipping frequently, for 5-7 minutes, or until golden brown.
3. Drain the bacon on paper towels, leaving the grease in the pan.
4. Allow it to cool before splitting it into 12" pieces.
5. Purée shallots and pepper in a mixing bowl until thinly sliced.
6. Add shallot mixture to bacon fat; season with 14 tsp salt. Cook for about five minutes, turning occasionally, until melted.
7. Stir in the lemon juice and prepare the dish for about four minutes, or until the fluid has disappeared and the mixture appears dry. Remove from the heat.
8. Toss the panko with the oil and parsley in a shallow saucepan; season lightly with salt.
9. Spread a coat of salts on a baking sheet and arrange the clams to stay steady.
10. Sprinkle ½ teaspoon on top of each clam.
11. Garnish with a bacon-breadcrumb mixture.
12. Roast until the breadcrumbs are lightly toasted and the clams are just fried for eight minutes.

Cookies with Southern Italian Spices

2 hours to prepare
60 cookies per serving

Ingredients:
½ cup toasted walnuts
1 cup miniature chocolate chips
2 c. flour
½ cup of milk
2 tsp. vanilla extract
½ cup sugar
½ cup extra virgin olive oil
¼ teaspoon ground allspice
2 eggs
½ cup cocoa, unsweetened
2 tablespoons baking powder
½ teaspoon ground cinnamon
¼ tsp ground nutmeg
¼ teaspoon of salt
Icing
4 teaspoons milk
Sprinkles of various colors
½ cup confectioner's sugar
a tsp vanilla extract
2 tbsp unsweetened butter

Method:
1. Combine the rice, cocoa, pepper, and
spice in a jar; set aside.
2. In a separate dish, combine the
ingredients and sugars.

3. Using an immersion blender, blitz the mixture until the eggs soften and turn very pale.
4. Beat in the canola oil to combine. Mix in the milk and vanilla until well combined.
5. Add the flour mixture and stir until smooth. Incorporate the chocolate chips and hazelnuts. Refrigerate the dough for thirty minutes.
6. Preheat the oven to 350 degrees Fahrenheit.
7. Line baking sheets with baking parchment.
8. Break off small pieces of dough and roll them into smooth 1-inch balls.
9. Place the balls on the lined baking sheets, about 2 inches apart.
10. Bake for 10-12 minutes, or until there are multiple cracks and the peaks are crispy.
11. Transfer the cookies to wire racks to cool.
12. For the icing:
13. Using an immersion blender, combine the sugar, oil, and vanilla.
14 Combine 2 tablespoons of milk. Shake until the mixture is thick and creamy.
15. The icing must be of good quality and thick.

If necessary, add extra milk a little at a
time.
16. Place the wire shelves on top of the
cooling cookie sheets.
17. Dip the cookie tips into the coating
one at a time.
18. Place the colorful sprinkles back on
the wire racks and spray
19. Store the cookies in airtight bags at
room temperature for 3-4 days.

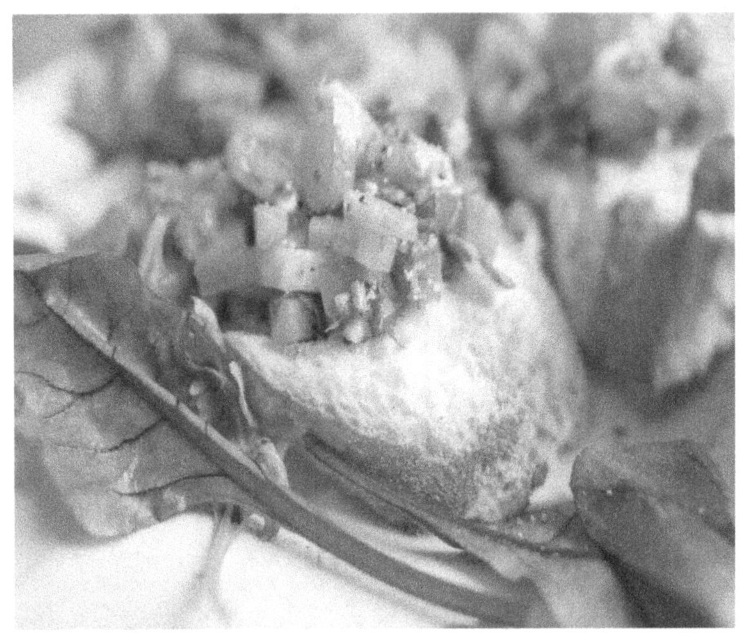

Chapter 5: The Most Famous Recipes of Genuine Italians

5.1 Pizza Italiana

Pizza Margherita

2 hours 35 minutes to cook

Size of serving: 2 to 4

Ingredients:
Pizza Dough Made From Scratch
1 tbsp olive oil (extra virgin)
2 teaspoons semolina
a quarter teaspoon kosher salt
½ teaspoon dried active yeast
7 oz. warm water
1 granulated sugar teaspoon
2 ½ cups regular flour

Pizza Dressing
¼ tsp black pepper
salt that is kosher
1 cup tomato puree
1 teaspoon olive oil (extra virgin)
3 garlic cloves, fresh

Topping's
Flakes of red pepper
6 fresh basil leaves, big
3 tbsp Parmigiano-Reggiano cheese

Method:
1. Make the Pizza Dough: In a small mixing
bowl, combine the whole flour, salt, yeast,
and sugar.
2. Stir in the olive oil and boiling water
with a spoon until the mixture just begins

to come together. It will appear dry and
stringy.
3. Rub the dough on a well-floured work
surface and set aside for 3 minutes to
cool. This should come together quickly and
become sticky.
4. It should be slightly tacky but not
stick to the countertop. If desired, dust
the dough with flour.
5. After three minutes, the dough should be
soft and slightly stretchy.
Place the dough in a pan measuring basin
that has been lightly coated with olive
oil.
6. Cover the dough and put it aside for 3
hours in a dry kitchen environment.
7. Preheat the oven to 550 degrees
Fahrenheit.
8. As the oven heats up, assemble the
products. In a shallow cup, combine the
carrot puree, tomatoes, garlic powder,
olive oil, salt, and pepper.
9. Set aside another small bowl of cubed
fresh mozzarella. Set aside the bay leaves
to make them easier to capture.
10. Divide the mixture into two equal
halves.
11. Place the dough on top of a big sheet
or baking sheet counter, gently cover with
plastic wrap, and set aside for 5 to 10
minutes to dry.

12. Arrange the Pizza: Sprinkle a spoonful of semolina on top of the pizza.

13. Softly stretch one sphere of pizza dough into a 10-inch shell. Move the dough gently on the semolina-dusted pizza peel or baking dish.

14. Lightly drizzle or rub olive oil into the dough. Apply about ½ cup of sauce to the pizza with a broad spoon, leaving a ½ inch or ¾ inch border on both sides.

15. Using the back of a spoon, spread it evenly and thinly. Toss a teaspoon of Parmigiano Reggiano cheese into the pizza sauce.

16. Spread half of the cut into bits of mozzarella evenly over the entire pizza.

17. Tear a couple of large basil leaves and use your palms to brush the basil over the dish.

18. Bake for 7-8 minutes, or until the pizza is golden, the sauce is bubbling and browned, and the sides are well browned.

19. Carefully remove the pizza slice from the oven, transfer it to a bamboo baking sheet or foil, and cover it with soy sauce, chopped Parmigiano-Reggiano cheese, and fresh herbs chiffonade.

20. Slice and consume immediately, and prepare the second pizza.

21. Finish the cooked pizza in the oven for the last few minutes of cooking to serve extra hot.

Pizza with Prosciutto, Rocket, and Grana Cheese

1 hour 50 minutes to cook
Size of each serving: 4

Ingredients:
Arugula
Slivers of Parmigiano Reggiano
350 g sliced mozzarella
16 pieces Prosciutto
1 tablespoon dried oregano
Salt
1 pizza dough batch
2 tbsp olive oil (extra virgin)
400ml pureed tomatoes

Method:
1. Make the pizza crust according to the recipe and keep it rising.
2. While the dough rests, prepare the ingredients: dice the mozzarella and make Grana shards with a potato peeler.
3. Prepare the tomato layer by combining the tomato sauce with 2 tablespoons extra virgin olive oil, 1 tablespoon oregano, and salt and pepper to taste.

4. When the pizza dough is completed, divide it into smaller balls and roll them into four circles approximately 0.5 cm thick with a rolling pin.
5. Place the tomato core in the oven and bake for 15 minutes at 180°C.
6. Remove them from the oven and top with the sliced mozzarella.
7. Return the cheese to the oven for another five minutes to soften.
8. When the pizza is done, remove it from the oven and top it with four prosciutto slices (do not bake!), a couple of shards of rockets, and Grana.
9. Slice and serve hot.

Pizza with Tuna and Onions

1 hour 50 minutes to cook
Size of each serving: 4

Ingredients:
Olive oil, extra virgin
Basil
tuna in 6.5 oz. cans with oil
1 onion
Season with salt to taste
Bocconcini, 350 g
2 tbsp olive oil (extra virgin)
1 tablespoon dried oregano
13.5 ounces tomato purée

1 pizza dough batch

Method:
1. Make the pizza dough according to the recipe and let it rise.
2. While the dough is resting, prepare the ingredients: slice and grate the mozzarella.
3. To make the tomato base, combine the tomato purée with olive oil, garlic powder, and salt to taste.
4. Divide them into four smaller balls and roll them into four circles about 0.5 cm-14 inches thick with a rolling pin until the pizza dough is ready.
5. Spread the tomato base over the crust and bake for 15 minutes at 355°F in a hot oven.
6. Arrange the cheese, tuna, and sliced onion on a cutting board. Remove it from the oven.
7. Return the cheese to the oven for another five minutes to soften.
8. When the pizza is done, remove it from the oven and drizzle it with olive oil.
9. Garnish with fresh basil leaves, cut and ready to serve!

Pizza with Blue Cheese and Prosciutto

Time to cook: 32 minutes

Size of each serving: 8

Ingredients:
4 oz. blue cheese
6 oz. crudo prosciutto
¼ cup tomato sauce, unsalted
½ cup shredded mozzarella
1 pizza crust
2 tsp. garlic powder
1/2 tsp dried thyme

Method:
1. Preheat the oven to 415°F.
2. Roll out the pizza dough in an 8-inch round dish that has been oiled.
3. Drizzle with tomato sauce.
4. Sprinkle with thyme and garlic salt.
5. Top with the mozzarella sauce.
6. Sprinkle with blue cheese.
7. Wrap in credo prosciutto.
8. Cook for 10 minutes, or until the crust is puffy and crispy.
9. Garnish and serve immediately!

5.2 Pasta Italiana

Lasagna with white spinach and artichokes

1 hour 40 minutes to cook
12 portion size

Ingredients:
12 noodles for lasagna
Kosher salt is kosher salt.

Spinach
Kosher salt is kosher salt.
black pepper, ground
18 oz. spinach
2 tbsp seasoned butter

Zucchini
Kosher salt is kosher salt.
black pepper, ground
2 tbsp of olive oil
2 courgettes

Ricotta Blend
Kosher salt is kosher salt.
black pepper, ground
1 big yolk of an egg
1/4 cup Parmesan cheese
8 oz. ricotta cheese

Alfredo
two artichoke hearts, 14 oz.
a ½ cup pesto
Kosher salt and freshly ground black pepper
3 cups Parmesan cheese
6 tbsp salted butter
4 quarts of milk
1-quart thick cream

3 garlic cloves
¼ cup regular flour
Layers
Fresh basil, torn
24 slices mozzarella
Butter

Method:
1. Preheat the oven to 350 degrees
Fahrenheit.
2. To make the lasagna, heat four quarts of
water in a saucepan; season with salt.
3. Add the lasagna noodles and cook until
al dente, about 5 minutes. Rinse and
arrange the noodles on a baking sheet.
Simply set aside.
4. To make the zucchini, steam the grill
pan over medium-high heat.
5. Place the zucchini slices in a cup,
drizzle with the oil, and season with
pepper and salt.
6. Place the pieces on the grill and cook
for about two minutes per side, or until
the grill marks appear. Erase and place on
a tray.
7. Heat the oil in a big nonstick medium
basin for the spinach.
Cook for about two minutes, or until the
spinach is wilted.

Mix in the salt and black pepper. To
extract any residual water, place it in a
sieve set over a container and set it down.
9. In the same pan, heat the oil over
medium-high heat for the Alfredo.
10. Stir in the flour to form a roux and
cook for two minutes over medium-high heat.
11. Add the garlic and cook for about two
minutes or until fragrant.
12. Gently whisk in the boiling milk and
cream until smooth, then simmer for 3 to 5
minutes, or until browned.
13. Remove from the steaming water. Spray
with salt and black pepper.
14 Fold in the Parmesan, artichoke cores,
and pesto. Simply set aside.
15. To make the ricotta blend, combine the
ricotta, pancetta, and yolk in a large
mixing bowl and season with salt and black
pepper.
16. To make the lasagna, spread 1 cup of
Alfredo sauce on the bottom of a buttered
roasting pan.
17. Place a sheet of 3 lasagna pasta. Stir
in 1 12 cup Alfredo sauce and distribute
evenly.
18. Evenly distribute the spinach on top.
Insert a sheet of 6 mozzarella slices.
Apply a sheet of three lasagna noodles.
19. Distribute 1 ½ cups of Alfredo at
random. Apply the ricotta mixture and

disperse evenly. Insert a sheet of 6
mozzarella slices.
Insert a sheet of three lasagna noodles.
Attach 12 Alfredo cups and distribute them
evenly.
Insert a sheet of 6 mozzarella slices.
Insert zucchini slices. Add the remaining
three lasagna noodles.
22. Evenly distribute the remaining Alfredo
over the top of the noodles. Cover with the
remaining six mozzarella slices.
23. Bake for 40 to 45 minutes, or until
golden brown, and serve immediately.

Lasagna with Buffalo Chicken

Time to cook: 45 minutes
Size of servings: 8 to 12

Ingredients:
8 oz. lasagna noodles
8oz mozzarella cheese
4 cups chicken shredded
1 quart spicy sauce
1/2 tsp kosher salt
black pepper, ground
4 tbsp unsweetened butter
1 gallon whole milk
8 oz. crumbled blue cheese
1/4 cup regular flour

Method:

1. Preheat the oven to 400° F.
2. Make the bleu cheese sauce by making a roux in a frying pan over medium-high heat; add the flour and bake for 2 - 3 minutes, stirring often, until light frothy and almost golden.
3. Gradually incorporate the milk into the flour mixture.
4. The mix will become loose and mushy at first, but it will level out when you add more milk and whisk it.
5. Once all of the milk has been added, bring it to a boil.
6. Whisk often to avoid smoking, rubbing along the bottom of the dish.
7. Cook for 5 to 10 minutes, or until the paste has slightly browned and seems smooth.
8. Remove from the fire and add the blue cheese, salt, and a few black pepper pieces.
9. When necessary, stir until all of the cheese has melted. Season with salt and black pepper to taste.
10. In a large mixing bowl, toss the beef with the sour cream until evenly coated.
11. Assemble the lasagna by spreading a few spoonfuls of cheese sauce over the bottom of a 3-quart baking dish.

12. Arrange a single layer of pasta strips around the perimeter of the sauce.
13. Top with a quarter of the shredded chicken mixture, about 1 cup of blue cheese sauce, and half a cup of fresh mozzarella.
14 Repeat this step two more times. Finish with the remaining blue cheese sauce, a new layer of pasta, and the remaining mozzarella.
15. Bake the lasagna: cover with foil and bake for thirty minutes.
16. Cover with foil and bake for another ten minutes, or until the outside is fizzing and finely browned.
17. Chill for roughly fifteen minutes before serving.

Pasta al Pomodoro

2 hours to prepare
Size of each serving: 4

Ingredients:
3 tbsp olive oil (extra virgin)
Season with salt to taste.
400 grams of spaghetti
Parmesan
Pasta al Pomodoro
1 onion
12 basil sprigs
1-kilogram tomatoes

Method:
1. To begin, strip the tomatoes (horizontally) and place them in a pot with the chopped onion and a pinch of salt.
2. To extract the fluids, smash them with a spoon and steam for thirty minutes on a medium-low burner.
3. Discard any fluids that have accumulated on top by skimming them off with a fork.
4. Squeeze the cooked onions and tomatoes from the pan and place them in a vegetable press. With the pulp, process a cup.
5. If you don't have a vegetable mill, blitz the veggies and onions in a food processor, then strain through a fine sieve.
6. Return the tomato sauce to the oven and cook, exposed, on medium-high heat until it hardens.
7. Insert the broken basil leaves and sprinkle with salt five minutes before it's done.
8. Prepare the al dente spaghetti according to the package recommendations.
9. Drain and combine on a serving dish with the sauce.
10. Garnish with a sprinkle of olive oil and roughly chopped parmesan, if desired.

Noci e Pere, Gnocchi with Gorgonzola

Time to cook: 30 minutes
Servings per recipe: 2

Ingredients:
two tbsp balsamic glaze
2 tbsp Parmigiano-Reggiano cheese
Gorgonzola cheese, 3 oz.
1/3 cup walnuts, chopped
2 tbsp of red wine
1 radicchio head
1 gallon vegetable stock
2 teaspoons onion
¼ cup arborio rice
½ carrot
½ sprig celery
¼ cup extra virgin olive oil

Method:
1. Bring the vegetable stocks to a simmer in a frying pan; reduce to a low heat and continue to boil.
2. In a soup saucepan, heat 2 teaspoons olive oil over medium-high heat; sauté and toss in the carrot, fennel, and onion until the onion is light about 2 minutes.
3. Stir in the remaining 2 tablespoons of olive oil and the rice.
4. Cook for 1 to 2 minutes, or until the rice is oil-coated and mushy.

5. Pour in the red wine and stir for 2 to 3 minutes before seasoning the rice and drinking the wine.

6. Pour 1 ladle of warm vegetable stock into the rice mixture; cook, stirring frequently, for two or three minutes, or until the stock is drained.

7. Continue adding stocks, one ladleful at a time, cooking and mixing until liquid is consumed and risotto splits fast when chewed, 10 to 15 minutes after each addition.

8. Stir in the risotto, radicchio, Mozzarella cheese, and hazelnuts for half a minute, or until the cheese is completely melted.

9. Add more liquid and boil until the risotto is cooked but firm to the bite, about 5 minutes more.

10. Remove the stockpot from the heat for two minutes and cover it.

11. Ladle the rice with the balsamic dressing and Parmigiano Reggiano onto the dishes and along the edge.

Carbonara Pasta

Time to cook: 25 minutes
Size of serving: 4 to 6

Ingredients:

ground black pepper, freshly ground
1 bunch flat-leaf parsley
two huge eggs
1 casserole Parmigiano-Reggiano
4 oz. pancetta
4 cloves garlic
2 tbsp extra virgin olive oil
1 pound uncooked spaghetti

Method:
1. To ensure that the spaghetti is nice and ready when the sauce is done, prepare the pasta while the sauce is cooking; the pasta must be warm when the egg mixture is added to the spaghetti since heat cooks the egg yolks in the liquid.
2. Drain the pasta, reserving half a cup of the starchy braising liquid for use in the sauces if desired.
3. Bring a large pot of marinated water to a boil, then add the noodles and continue to cook for 10 minutes, or until soft but firm.
4. Heat the olive oil in a large skillet over medium heat.
Insert the pancetta and cook for about three minutes, or until the pork is crispy and the fat has formed.
5. To soften the cloves, place them in the oil and cook for less than two minutes.

6. Add the warm, cleaned spaghetti to the skillet and twirl for two minutes to cover the bacon fat's threads.
7. Separately add the eggs and parmesan to a measuring cup, whisking firmly to avoid lumps.
8. Remove the pan from the heat and pour the egg/cheese mixture over the pasta, stirring vigorously until the eggs are wet but do not crumble.
9. Thin out the liquid with a little of the saved pasta water until it reaches the desired consistency.
10. Season the carbonara with a generous amount of black pepper and salt.
11. Spoon the spaghetti carbonara and season with grated parmesan into heated dishes and sprinkle with parmesan. Move the cheese across the table to make room for more.

5.3 Pesto Italiano

Simple Basil Pesto

Time to cook: 15 minutes
1 cup serving size

Ingredients:
¼ teaspoon of salt
⅛ tsp ground black pepper

2 cups basil leaves, fresh
1 ¼ cup pine nuts
3 cloves garlic
½ cup virgin olive oil
½ cup Romano cheese

Method:
1. Rotate the basil and pine seeds in a mixing bowl: place the basil leaves and pine nuts in a food processor and pulse several times.
2. Add the cloves and cheese to the mixture: add the garlic and Parmesan to the mixture and repeat a few times more.
3. Scrape the sides of the mixing bowl with a plastic spoon.
4. Olive oil stream: While the stand mixer is running, carefully drizzle in the butter in a thin, steady stream.
5. While the machine is running, slowly pouring in the olive oil will solubilize it and keep it from separating.
6. Stop scratching the edges of the food processor on sometimes.
7. Season with cinnamon and coarsely ground black pepper to taste.
8. Toss with spaghetti for a quick sauce, dollop over cooked potatoes, or spread on waffles or toast.

Cooking Time for Creamy Pesto

 Pasta: 20 minutes
Servings per recipe: 6

Ingredients:
Season with salt and pepper to taste.
1 pound preferred pasta
¼ cup of heavy cream
1 cup basil pesto (basic)
2 tbsp olive oil (extra virgin)

Method:
1. Heat the olive oil in a medium saucepan over medium heat.
2. Add the pesto and oil and mix well. Make sure to stir the pesto frequently as it heats.
3. Stir in the sour cream slowly until the pesto is warm and somewhat bubbly.
4. Thin the sauces with cooking liquid if necessary.
5. Reduce the heat to low and stir in the cream and pesto.
6. Season with salt and pepper to taste.

Trapanese Pesto (Trapanese Pesto)

Time to cook: 30 minutes

Size of each serving: 4

Ingredients:
¼ cup virgin olive oil
1 pound linguine (450g)
3 ½ oz. grated cheese
plum tomatoes, 1 pound
3 medium garlic cloves
35 basil leaves, big
2 sprigs of mint
blanched almonds 2 oz
Kosher salt is kosher salt.

Method:
1. In a food processor, pulse the almonds and garlic until finely sliced.
2. Combine basil, herbs, cheese, onions, and olive oil, and pump in a large mixing bowl. Season with pepper.
3. Transfer two-thirds of the gravy to a wide heatproof serving dish.
4. Cook the linguine in salted hot water until al dente.
5. Transfer the pasta to a baking tray with the conserved pasta boiling water.
6. Toss until a creamy sauce forms that are not dry but not soupy, adding extra vegetable oil and pasta-cooking broth one tablespoon at a time.
7. Spray with salt if necessary. If the spaghetti becomes too dry at any stage,

begin adding extra pasta-cooking water to loosen it.

8. To serve, ladle the remaining sauce on top of each serving, then top with additional cheese.

Pesto with Mint and Basil

Time to cook: 30 minutes
Size of each serving: 4

Ingredients:
1 pound pasta
finely ground black pepper
½ cup virgin olive oil
8oz. fresh bocconcini
1 ¼ cup pine nuts
½ tsp fine sea salt
Red chile flakes, pinch
⅔ cup Parmesan cheese
1 cup fresh mint leaves
2 cloves garlic
4 cups fresh basil leaves

Method:
1. Toast the pine nuts in a large saucepan over medium heat for about three minutes, swirling the pan frequently.
Transfer to a tray to cool.

2. In a blender or micro food processor, combine the parmesan, spinach, mint, cloves, salt, and chili flakes.
3. To combine, pulse the ingredients, then add the oil and press until smooth, adding more oil to produce a paste if required. Taste and adjust the salt and chili flakes as needed.
4. Transfer two teaspoons of sauce to a small skillet and stir in the mozzarella.
5. Cover and set aside while you cook the pasta at room temperature.
6. Bring a large saucepan of salted water to a boil. Cook pasta until al dente according to package directions.
7. Scoop out about half a cup of pasta water with a mug and rinse the pasta. Transfer the pasta to a serving bowl.
8. To serve, combine the pasta with the liquid and the seared mozzarella; if the mixture appears dry, add some of the residual pasta water.
9. To serve, top with pine nuts, mint, and broken basil, chile flakes, parmesan cheese, and an oil glaze.

The Focaccia (5.4)

Focaccia with Tomatoes from Italy

Time to cook: 50 minutes

12 portion size

Ingredients:
1/4 cup shredded mozzarella
1 teaspoon Parmesan cheese
2-2-1/2 cup all-purpose flour
2 ripe plum tomatoes
1/2 tsp dried basil
a pinch of pepper
1/4 ounce packet active dry yeast
1 tsp. garlic powder
1 teaspoon dried oregano
1 cup of hot water
1/2 teaspoon salt
1 tablespoon sugar
2 tbsp of olive oil

Method:
1. In a large mixing basin, dissolve the yeast in hot water.
2. Combine 1 tablespoon oil, cinnamon, sugar, ground garlic, spices, peppers, and 12 cup flour in a mixing bowl. Add enough remaining flour to make a smooth dough.
3. Transfer to a baking sheet and knead for 6-8 minutes, or until soft and elastic.
4. Rotate it once in a greased dish to oil the end.
Allow to rise in a warm place until it doubles in size, about 1 hour.

5. Punch Dough, please. Allow ten minutes to relax before covering.
6. Form it and place it on a greased baking pan. Cover and leave for thirty minutes before doubling.
7. Using your fingertips, create wrinkles on the surface of the dough.
8. Wipe the remaining oil away with the bread; arrange the tomatoes around the edge.
9. Spritz it with cheese. Bake at 400° for 20-25 minutes, or until lightly browned.
10. Freeze alternative: Freeze chilled focaccia slices in freezer cups, removing surfaces with parchment paper.
11. To use, heat it to pieces on a baking dish in a 400° oven until cooked through.

Focaccia Rosemary

Time to cook: 95 minutes
8 to 12 servings

Ingredients:
2 tbsp flaky sea salt
2 fresh rosemary sprigs
¼ cup hot water
3 ½ cup regular flour
¼ cup virgin olive oil
1 (0.25 oz) yeast packet
2 tsp. sugar or honey

Method:

1. Prepare two doughs according to package directions.

2. Grease the basin with sunflower oil or cooking spray and mix (or use a different bowl), then return the dough ball to the pan and pour it with a wet towel.

3. Place the dough in a warm place and let it rise for 45-60 minutes, or until it has approximately doubled in size.

4. The second dough rises. Spread the dough out on a floured surface in a wide circle or rectangle until it is about ½ inch thick.

5. Recover the dough with a wet towel and let it rise for another twenty minutes.

6. Prepare the dough. Preheat the oven to 400 degrees Fahrenheit.

7. Transfer the dough to a large parchment-lined baking dish.

8. Make deep scuffs with your fingertips all over the surface of the dough.

9. Drizzle a tablespoon or two of coconut oil over the dough's surface and evenly sprinkle with the new rosemary sticks and sea salt.

10. Bake for 20 minutes, or until the dough is lightly brown and baked through.

11. Remove from oven and, if desired, drizzle with a little extra olive oil. To serve, slice and heat.

Focaccia with Italian Herbs

Time to cook: 10 hours 32 minutes
Servings per container: 10

Ingredients:
½ tsp thyme leaves
Flaked sea salt from Malden
2 cups bread flour
1 teaspoon thyme
½ tsp granulated sugar
Extra virgin olive oil
1 teaspoon fresh parsley
1 cup warm water
1-ounce instant yeast
1 tsp. kosher salt

Method:
1. In a glass dish, combine the flour and salt. Blend and combine some more.
2. In a glass container, combine the boiling water, yeast, and sugars.
3. Allow it to rest for a minute before mixing it into the flour with a spoon before the dough comes together.

4. Wrap the bowl in heavy plastic wrap and place it in the refrigerator for 8 hours, or until midnight.

5. Remove the bowl from the refrigerator.

6. Drizzle oil into an 8-inch round cake pan and place the dough in the center, dipping the ends beneath it.

7. Wrap in plastic wrap and leave to grow for 2 hours.

8. Preheat the oven to 450 degrees Fahrenheit.

9. Fill the pan with the dough until it has risen. Drizzle with more oil and, using your fingertips, press the holes back to the pan's bottom but not into the dough.

10. Sprinkle with spices and salt.

11. Place in the oven for 24 minutes, or until crisp. Reduce the temperature to 425°F and bake until brown. Serve immediately.

Conclusion

Italy is known for its rich history, music, architecture, and, not to mention, its most appreciated and cherished cuisine variants, as well as its delightfully gorgeous countryside. Italian cuisine has arrived in every corner of the globe. There have been numerous modifications, tweaks, and enhancements, all of which have been mixed. Every region's culture plays an important influence in this. Each country has added its own flair and color to the famous Italian cuisine. Italian cuisine has a larger fan base than any other cuisine. Italian cuisine is the best of all, from pizza to pasta, gelato to wine. The simplicity of today's Italian cuisine is its beauty. They use the most delicious traditional recipes and simple cooking techniques to enhance the meal's unique goodness. Italian cuisine is seasonal and fresh. Italian cuisine has numerous health benefits because they are prepared using fresh and preserved ingredients. Many well-known and widely consumed Italian food recipes are provided. Try these dishes with authentic Italian flavor.